Be Still & Know That
I Am God

Dr. Michael Alton II

ISBN 978-1-0980-4729-0 (paperback)
ISBN 978-1-0980-4730-6 (digital)

Christian Faith Publishing, Inc.
832 Park Avenue
Meadville, PA 16335
www.christianfaithpublishing.com

Printed in the United States of America

Presented To

By

Date

Foreword

The purpose of this book is to show God's faithfulness to his word and to give hope for those who are struggling and going through trials and tribulations. It is a true story of God's miracles that were given to me because I chose to believe and have faith in my father in heaven and his only son, Jesus Christ, and the words that they spoke to me. God showed me abundant grace and mercy at the lowest point in my life and further established my faith and trust in his word, Jesus Christ.

Acknowledgments

I want to thank Father God for choosing me to show his love for mankind and allowing me to experience firsthand, your supernatural gifts of healing and miracles. Thank you, Father God, for trusting me to fight the good fight and be your servant so that others may come to know your son Jesus Christ. Thank you, Father God, for the grace you gave me and allowed me to live when I should not have. Thank you, Father God, for the mercy you showed me when I was in horrible pain and felt as if I could die at any second, but you kept me close next to you and comforted me.

I want to thank Jesus Christ for being my Lord and Savior. Thank you for loving us and enduring all that you did and dying for our sins.

I want to thank the Holy Spirit for being with me every step of the way and speaking with me and showing me God's truth. You revealed so much to me that I was unaware of. Thank you for not giving up on me even when I wanted to give up.

I want to thank my son, Michael David Alton III, for having to be strong at such a young age and witness his dad go through cancer treatments. My son was fortunate enough to see firsthand God's miracles at work.

I want to thank my parents and family for being my caregivers. I want to thank them for being strong when I know their hearts were breaking by seeing one of their children having leukemia and going through everything that comes along with it.

I want to thank the Veterans Administration, Baylor Scott and White hospitals, and Vanderbilt hospital for everything that you do to make a positive experience and be a beacon of light and hope in the lives of people who are counting on you.

I want to thank the tens of thousands of people who were praying for me. Your prayers were heard, and God surely answered them.

Thank you, Thomas Gross, a.k.a. Thom Barry, for being part of my wise counsel over the past twenty years. Thank you for the long phone calls that averaged three hours each. Thank you for sharing the wisdom that God has given you.

"**G**od said, 'You are not going to die from this my child. You can quit crying now.'"

It was December 2013, and I was at Gold's Gym foam rolling my back after my workout. Usually, this would feel really good, but I noticed it was hurting my spine. No matter where I placed the foam roller, it would hurt my vertebrae. I had worked out with weights from the age of eight and was in great physical shape, so I chalked this up to nothing and figured it would go away on its own. The pain was only minimal, and after a few months of it being there every time I use the foam roller, I figured this was just the new norm.

I graduated from Cleveland Chiropractic College of Los Angeles in 2002 and had been practicing in Austin, Texas, since 2005. It was now February 2014 and my practice was doing well. A colleague of mine, Dr. Simon Forster, owned the building where my clinic was located, and we shared office staff. It was a fantastic set up as Dr. Forster rented space to several other medical doctors including pain management, allergies, and ob-gyn.

It was around this time that I began having lower neck pain. I had asked Dr. Forster to give me a spinal adjustment to see if it would help. After the adjustment, I lost 50 percent of the strength in my left arm and immediately went and had an MRI of the cervical spine. After the MRI, I went to Gold's Gym for my daily workout. I was on the elliptical machine when I received a phone call from the MRI facility. It was the radiologist calling to give me my report. He stated that it is never good when the radiologist calls the same day to give the report. My heart began racing as I anticipated what he was about to say. I was thinking, *How bad could it be if he is calling the same day?* He said he noticed several infiltrates in every vertebrae in my neck. He said this was probably nothing but that I should have further evaluation because it could be several different diseases including cancer. I was in such good shape, so I dismissed his recommendation on being further evaluated, and I really only heard him say that it was probably nothing.

A month went by and one Sunday morning, I awoke to a swollen left ankle. The funny thing is that it was not painful at all. Just to be safe, I had an ultrasound performed at my local VA hospital to determine the cause. The results were negative for a blood clot, and in a few days, the swelling subsided and completely went away.

It was now April. Austin, Texas, is known as the allergy capital of the world and yellow pollen covered everything. I had developed a cough and noticed tiny specks of blood in my sputum. Once again, I thought nothing of it and figured it was due to cedar fever or one of the several other allergens in the air.

The following month, I awoke to another left swollen ankle, but this time, it was excruciatingly painful. It was so swollen and painful, I thought my skin was going to tear open. I called my father and he took me to the emergency room. I explained to the doctors that this was the second time in a few months that I had had a swollen ankle and that I had also been coughing up tiny specks of blood. They decided to perform a CT scan of my lungs and an ultrasound of my left leg. The ultrasound concluded that I did in fact have a blood clot in my left lower leg. The CT scan revealed that my lungs were saturated with blood clots and that my right lower lobe had an infarct.

I was immediately started on heparin to control blood clot formation and was closely monitored in the hospital over the next couple of days. When I was released from the hospital, the plan was to have blood work every other day to monitor my progress.

My blood work showed a falling trend. My red blood cell count, hematocrit, and platelets all began to drop. The doctors thought it was due to Heparin Induced Thrombocytopenia (HIT) so they switched my blood thinning medication to Coumadin. Over the next couple of weeks, my blood values continued to dramatically drop. I began having difficulty breathing, shortness of breath, and lightheadedness upon physical exertion.

It was June, Friday the thirteenth, 2014, and I had just arrived at my clinic. My clinic was on the second floor, and it was always quicker to take the stairs as opposed to the elevator. Halfway up the stairs, I had to stop and bend over to catch my breath. After I had reached the top of the stairs, I had to take another minute break to catch my breath before continuing on to my clinic. I felt as if I was going to pass out. It was at this time I realized something was dramatically wrong and I felt that I might die that day. I walked into my clinic and asked the front desk supervisor to cancel all my patients. I explained to her that something was very wrong and that I was going to the ER. I called my father and he took me to the Central Texas VA Hospital in Temple, Texas.

I was introduced to Dr. Juan Posada, the chief oncologist at the Central Texas VA hospital. He performed my first bone marrow biopsy. Two days later was Father's Day and it fell on a Sunday. That evening, my hematologist came to see me. He said, "You know it is never good when your doctor comes to give you your diagnosis late on a Sunday evening." My heart started racing. I knew that the diagnosis was going to be bad, but I did not know how bad. I was hoping he was not going to say that I only had a short time to live. He explained that I had two types of leukemia, acute lympho-blastic leukemia pre-B cell type and acute myelogenous leu-kemia. He said 60 percent of my bone marrow throughout my body was cancerous. When he left, I walked outside and sat underneath the American flag and prayed fervently.

Let us therefore come boldly unto the throne of grace, that we may obtain mercy, and find grace to help in time of need. (Hebrews 4:16)

The next day, I was started on an aggressive chemother-apy regimen called HyperCVAD part A. I was also started on intrathecal spinal injections of Methotrexate chemotherapy. The Methotrexate was injected into the spinal fluid between the third and fourth lumbar vertebrae. Once the chemother-apy was in my spinal fluid, it would cross the blood brain barrier and bathe my brain. My chemotherapies target and kill the blood, including all cells in the blood and bone mar-row. Once the chemotherapy has taken effect, I reached a point called the Nadir. This is the point where a patient has no immune system due to the lack of white blood cells to fight off infections. This was a very vulnerable point, and I took several precautions not to get sick. My room in the hospital was a negative pressure room. Filtered air is pumped into the room and would be pushed out of the door so when staff would enter the room, no pathogens would be sucked into the room, rather they would have been blown out.

During my stay in the hospital, I thanked God over and over for allowing me to experience this trial. Not once did I ever say, "Why me." The way I saw was "Why not me." I had given my life to Christ at age twelve. I knew that being a Christian meant I would increase my faith through trials and tribulations.

One day, I was watching television and the actor Will Smith was being interviewed. He was explaining how he created his life path by thinking positive thoughts and creating his future. He said he read a book by Paulo Cuelho called *The Alchemist* that changed his life. A few days later, I saw Will Smith and Tyrese Gibson on television and they both were talking about the book *The Alchemist*. I saw this as a sign from God and downloaded *The Alchemist* and read it at once. It was a great read and helped me understand that I was in control of my destiny. I ended up reading all of Paulo Cuelho's books.

I also watched a lot of television during these months in the hospital. My favorite channel was Trinity Broadcasting Network. I loved listening to several preachers like Creflo Dollar, Joyce Meyer, Dr. David Jeremiah, Joel Osteen, John Hagee, and Charles Stanley. They preach positive and uplifting sermons. They all spoke life into me through the word of God. Watching them daily was a true blessing. Even though I was at the lowest point in my life, God gave me a sense of peace that surpasses all understanding.

After the first month, my hair was getting a little long, and I would pull on my sideburns because it bothered me that they were so long. I was just slightly tugging on them and one entire sideburn pulled completely out of the side of my head. It did not hurt at all. I reached up and tugged on the hair on top of my head and it came out with little effort as well. I found this amusing and began laughing. My son and his mother were visiting me that day and they asked why I was laughing. I pulled another clump of hair out and showed them. My son was six at the time and could not understand how I was able to do this without pain. It scared him and he began to cry. Children are so innocent at that age. I immediately picked him up and hugged him and let him know everything was going to be alright. That was a good lesson for me. What was humorous for me was very scary for him.

It took a while for my immune system and bone marrow to regenerate. I ended up staying in the hospital for three months until my immune system was reestablished. At this point, I had another bone marrow biopsy performed at to determine if the chemotherapy had been effective. When the results to come back, it was determined that the leukemia had grown, and I now had 70 to 80 percent cancer in the bone marrow. My oncologist told me not to worry and doubt we would be starting the most aggressive chemotherapy known to fight leukemia and it was called HyperCVAD part B. I also continued receiving the intrathecal Methotrexate injections.

After the new chemotherapy took effect, the Nadir was a little tougher to handle. My red blood cell count was two-thirds low and I had very little energy. My son had to push me in a wheelchair because I had no energy to stand up and walk. My back was hurting from lying in bed for weeks, and I would have given anything to have a chiropractic adjustment and a massage. I had zero platelets in my blood to stop any bleeding that may occur. I was not allowed to brush my teeth in order to prevent any blood loss from my gums. If I ate too large of a meal, I would be on the verge of passing out because of the low blood volume I had in my body would accumulate in the gut for digestion. I quickly learned to eat very small meals. Another effect of having no platelets was the inability of my body to close the hole in my spine after having a Methotrexate injection. This allowed the fluid in my spine to leak out. This fluid leak caused a horrible and incapacitating headache if I was in an upright position. If I was lying flat, I had no headache. Doctors correct this leak by applying a blood patch to the area. I was not a candidate for this procedure due to the possibility of introducing the leukemia cells into my spinal fluid. This headache lasted twenty-six days and finally resolved after my nurse anointed my head with holy oil and prayed over me which I will discuss later in this chapter.

After a few weeks of finishing the HyperCVAD part B, my red and white blood cell count began to rise, and the hospital allowed me to go home to recover. My mother had put her job on hold and moved in with me to be my full-time caregiver. It was so nice to be home around my family. There was not any hospital alarm sounds continually going off. There was no one checking on my status every couple of hours. Even though I still had the horrible spinal headache. If I sat upright, it was still better experiencing it at home as apposed to being in the hospital. It was a peaceful time which allowed me to get uninterrupted sleep and well-needed healing.

I had been at home recovering for three weeks when I woke up one morning and felt hot and I knew something was not right. I took Tylenol and laid back down and waited for it to take effect. After thirty minutes, I began to feel a little better. I remembered my oncology team saying if I get a temperature of 100.4 degrees or higher, I need to immediately come to the hospital. I took my temperature and it was 100.7 degrees. I also knew that the Tylenol had taken effect and that my temperature was actually higher than the reading I had just taken. I was reluctant to tell my mother because that meant I was going back to the hospital. After I explained the situation to her, we packed up and headed out. I had to lay down in the back seat due to the spinal headache. During the ride to the hospital, I began having uncontrollable shaking known as rigors. I was so weak because of chemotherapy and now my body was violently shivering and contracting uncontrollably and using what little energy I had left. It felt like my body was trying to kill itself. Once in the ER, I was covered with several warm blankets. I remember counting ten blankets and that still was not enough to make me feel warm even though I was burning up. An hour passed and the ER doctor finally gave me a sedative called Versed. It was a godsend. I immediately quit shivering. This occurred just in time as I could not have endured the rigors any longer. My body would have died due to lack of energy. That morning, once I stabilized, I was transferred to a level one trauma hospital that could accommodate my needs.

My blood work revealed that a gram-positive bacterium called *Streptococcus viridans* had infiltrated my body through my PICC line and my blood was septic. My doctor explained that he was starting me on the most powerful antibiotic they had in order to get control of the septicemia. He also explained that the powerful antibiotic could possibly kill me as well as my septic blood. He said that if there was ever a time to fight for my life, it was now. He said the probability of surviving the night was not good. My entire body was swollen with inflammation and my organs were shutting down. The doctor brought in the surgical team to discuss putting a drain in my gallbladder to reduce the inflammation. I told the doctor that if I was not any better the next day, to go ahead with the surgery.

That night, my parents came to see me and give their blessings and prayers. My mother prayed the blood of Jesus over me and they went home to prepare for the next day. I was now alone and began thinking about my situation. How am I supposed to fight for my life? I was so weak and was afraid to go to sleep for fear of dying. I could barely move from lack of energy and just breathing was difficult enough. I began thinking about my family and friends that had passed away. At that moment, I came to grips with dying. I rationalized it by knowing we all are going to die. After all, I did make it to forty-one years of age and had led a great life.

I felt the sense of death around me. Death has an unforgettable presence and I was very aware of it. I was not afraid, and the feeling of death was not dark or gloomy. At that moment, the Holy Spirit spoke to me and said, "Here is death. It is right here before you. It is not something to be afraid of. It is actually peaceful. All you have to do is step through it." I thanked the Holy Spirit for talking to me and making me feel at ease with crossing through it. The Holy Spirit then questioned me about why I was worried. I explained that I was worried about what was going to happen to my son and who was going to raise him. I wondered if he was going to be okay. The Holy Spirit reminded me that God had already saved me several times throughout my life when I would make bad decisions and do very dangerous and stupid things. He assured me that God is more than capable of making sure that my son is well taken care of. That is when I realized I was not trusting God with everything. I immediately asked for forgiveness for not trusting God completely. At that exact moment, I gave God complete control over everything. I thanked him for loving me and let him know I was in his hands to do with whatever he wished. A great weight was suddenly lifted off my shoulders and I was at peace. I didn't have to fight any longer. God would fight for me and do it whichever way he chose. Whether it to bring me home to heaven or allow me to stay on earth, I was just fine either way.

Exodus14:14 says, "The Lord will fight for you; you need only to be still."

I fell asleep quickly and slept all night. When I woke up the next morning, I was grateful to still be on earth. The inflammation in my gut had subsided and there was no pain. The surgical team came in and was expecting to place a drain tube in my gallbladder. They seemed a little disappointed when I explained I was feeling much better and that I did not need the surgery. Over the next two weeks, I continued to improve. I still had the spinal headache if I sat up, but life was much better.

While in the hospital, I explained to the nurse that I had a spinal headache from a lumbar puncture in order to infuse chemotherapy into my spinal fluid so it could cross the blood brain barrier and bathe my brain. The spinal fluid had continued to leak out because I had no platelets in my blood to form a clot and close the puncture site. It is an inde-scribable headache and can only be alleviated by lying flat on your back. At this point, the headache had lasted twenty-six days. She asked if she could anoint my head and pray for me. I gladly said yes. She reached into her pocket and pulled out a vial of holy water. She anointed my head and laid hands on me and began to pray out loud and in tongues. Immediately, I was covered in the Holy Spirit. It was like I was wrapped in a warm fuzzy and all my hair stood on end. It was a fantastic feeling of love. Tears started to run down the sides of my face. The tears felt so hot, I thought they may burn my skin. The tears continued to pour out and I could feel sickness leaving my body. I had never experienced something like that, and it was wonderful. After the nurse completed her prayer, I sat up and the spinal headache was completely gone. It was a miracle. God's peace covered me. After a few weeks in the hospital, I was able to go back home.

The time had come to have another bone marrow biopsy to determine if the last chemotherapy treatments had been effective in killing the leukemia. I had the biopsy and returned to the hospital a week later to hear the results. I had been feeling better lately so I drove myself to meet with my oncology team. This was a teaching hospital, so my oncologist gathered all the resident doctors in a room and brought me in. He explained that I unfortunately did not respond to the chemotherapy and that I now had 90 percent cancer in my bone marrow. He said I was going to die and that I needed to tell my son and my remaining family members. He told me to get my finances in order and pick out the music for my funeral. This was a shock to me because I was feeling much better and could have sworn the chemotherapy was working. I had been going back to the gym daily and getting stronger. In my disbelief, I asked him how I was going to die. He said I was going to die from an infection or disseminated intravascular coagulation (DIC), which is a condition affecting the body's ability to stop internal bleeding. Lastly, my doctor said he was surprised I am still alive and that it is hard to believe the leukemia has not spread and turned into a wild fire. He ended the death speech by saying the hospital was releasing me to go be with my family and enjoy what time I had left on earth. This was a hard pill to swallow. Here I was feeling much better, but I was actually on the verge of death.

"For with God nothing shall be impossible." (Luke 1:37)

The drive home took an hour and gave me plenty of time to think. All I could think about was my son and how his life would be without me. I knew God was going to take great care of him, but I was still greatly saddened and was sobbing nonstop. My heart was broken. I was at an all-time low. That is the exact moment when God spoke to me. It was the most gentle, fatherly voice you could ever imagine.

He said, "You are not going to die from this my child. You can quit crying now." Immediately, I came to my senses and realized what just happened. God had singled me out and spoke directly to me. I was filled with immense wonderful joy and began crying even harder. It was such a great feeling of relief. I knew I wasn't going to die. God engulfed me with his love. It was an intensely good feeling of warm pressure all over my body, and once again, my hair stood on end. It was like being wrapped in an indescribable warm fuzzy of white light. My entire body tingled and felt like it had never felt before. It was magnificent. When God speaks to you, you will know. There is no second-guessing. My outlook on life had been restored. I was so grateful to be alive and know that I was not going to die.

Being released from the hospital gave me lots of time to get my body back in shape. I couldn't wait to get back in the gym and start working out. I was extremely weak from the chemotherapy coupled with lying in bed for three months. I would be short of breath just going from a seated to a standing position. I started training with very light weights every day and sitting in the sauna to sweat out toxins. The first time I trained legs I used a forty-five-pound plate on each side of the bar and did four sets of squats for ten repetitions each. I left the gym feeling light headed and thought that I might have over done it a bit. The next day, I developed a pain in my left buttocks that traveled down my leg. If I laid down, the pain would go away. As the week progressed, my leg pain became worse and I started noticing subtle changes in all of my senses. I was hearing things that actually were not happening. In one ear, I would hear the sounds of locusts, and in the other ear, I would hear the sounds of rushing waters. When I laid down, I would see dark figures on the ceiling dancing around. I had the constant taste of metal no matter what I ate. I smelled dog feces throughout the day even though there was none. It felt like spiders and ants were crawling on my legs even though they weren't. I had horrible sciatic pain down my left leg. I was experiencing all of these at the same time. I explained my situation to my oncologist, and he ordered MRIs for my brain, neck, upper and lower back areas. The results showed that I had three areas where my brain was bleeding. My oncologist said this was occurring because my blood vessels were brittle and weak from the chemotherapy and had ruptured in my brain during my weight training sessions. Needless to say, I stopped weight training and just focused on eating heathy. Over time, my brain healed, and everything returned back to normal.

My son and I were both members of Gracie Barra Jujitsu in Cedar Park, Texas, and had been attending classes for a year before I was diagnosed with leukemia. Now that I was back home, this meant I could take my son to jujitsu again. Gracie Barra is not just about jujitsu. It is about family and taking care of everyone in class who has different needs. The team members took very good care of my son while I was gone and still do to this day. On Saturdays, world champion, Professor Fabio Villela, the owner of Gracie Barra in Cedar Park, would have his students meet at a park for exercise instead of the studio. Professor Fabio always looked out for my son Michael and watched over him when I could not be there. The park was big and wide open with trees surrounding the perimeter. The class was being held in the center of the park. As I was watching the class perform exercises, a man approached me. He said that he could tell that I had cancer. After all, I was now bald and withered due to the effects of chemotherapy. I explained to him that I had two types of leukemia and that I had already tried all known adult chemotherapies and that they had failed. He asked me if I had heard of vitamin B-17.

He said it was also called Laetril. I said no and he said I would check it out if I were you. I reached into my pocket to get my phone so I could send myself a text of the names. When I looked up to thank the gentleman, he was gone, nowhere to be found. Remember, this was a wide-open park and I should have been able to at least see him. I knew this was a messenger from God and that I needed to investigate vitamin B-17. When I got home, I looked it up online and discovered it was the derivative of arsenic. I was able to order it from a pharmacy in Mexico. The pharmacy had labelled it Novodalin. I began taking it immediately upon arrival. I took 500 mg twice a day, and some days, I would double or triple the dose just to see how I would feel. When I did this, I would feel sick, like I might have overdosed.

I had been taking Novodalin for a month when I received a call from the Vanderbilt/VA hospital. They offered to try the pediatric chemotherapies known to treat leukemia. They explained that the pediatric chemotherapies were stronger than the adult chemotherapies and that there was a good chance that I might die due to the side effects. Knowing that I was not going to die, I accepted the offer. I flew to Nashville a week later to begin the treatment. Before treatment, I had another bone marrow biopsy to determine the amount of leukemia in the marrow. When the results came back, the leukemia had dropped from 90 percent to 30 percent. I did not tell my oncologist that I had been taking vitamin B-17. I asked my team how this could have happened, and they did not know. They guessed it may have been from delayed effects of the adult chemotherapy.

The next day, I was started on the pediatric chemotherapy regimen. This was a very difficult time for me as the effects seemed so much worse than the adult chemotherapies. I felt as if I could die at any moment and this lasted for weeks. I had to remind myself on several occasions that God said I was not going to die from this. Satan tried to get me to second-guess God's word to me when I was at my lowest and felt my worst. It was up to me to believe what God had said and know that this difficult time would eventually pass. My entire body ached, and I was more miserable than I ever had been. I knew if the chemotherapy had positive effects, I would have to go through another round. I broke down and prayed beggingly to Jesus to please take this disease from me so I would not have to go through another round of chemotherapy. Suddenly, as clear as day, Jesus spoke to me and said, "Will you go through it for me?" I immediately responded and said, "Yes, Jesus, I will." Once again, when God speaks to you, you will know it. I changed my attitude and got mentally prepared for another round of chemotherapy.

I was given another bone marrow biopsy before starting the next round of chemotherapy to determine if the first round of pediatric chemotherapy had been effective. When the results came back, it was determined the chemotherapy had been ineffective and my marrow was still 30 percent cancerous. She said there was no reason to continue the second round. Even though it had failed, it was a great blessing for me knowing that I would not have any more pediatric chemotherapy. I was willing to go through it for Jesus, but he showed me mercy and did not allow it. Thank you, Jesus.

My father was my caregiver during the pediatric chemotherapy treatments. I lived in the VA/Vanderbilt hospital and he lived in an apartment across from the hospital. I was missing my son, so my stepmother Jill and my brother Travis drove my son from Austin to Nashville to see me. My brother drove the entire thirteen hours in one trip so I could see my baby boy. God bless him for that. It was so good to see everyone even though I was very miserable. Seeing them brought life into my body and raised my spirits. I loved snuggling with my son, and that is the first thing we did when they arrived.

The next day, I was supposed to meet them in the Vanderbilt cafeteria for lunch. I wasn't feeling well and wanted to get lunch and head back to my room. I was worried about being around so many people in the cafeteria because I was immunocompromised and could not afford to get sick. They were running late, and I began to get annoyed. I tried calling, but there was no answer. After a while, my brother came running in the cafeteria doors and grabbed some napkins and ran back out. I suddenly became worried and went after him. When I found them, my brother was holding my son who was crying, and Jill was attending to my father who was holding his arm that was covered in blood. I was so worried and asked what happened. My son wanted to race my dad to the cafeteria and when doing so, tripped over my dad and began to fall onto the pavement. My dad sacrificed his body to catch my son from hitting the concrete. He caught my son in his arms, and they both feel to the ground. My dad's arms took the brunt of the fall and were bleeding badly. My son had no injuries and was crying because it scared him. Luckily, we were at a fantastic hospital and the nurses took great care of my dad.

The following day, my father returned home to Austin with my stepmother, my brother, and my son. My mother and sister Holly drove in that day to be my caregivers. The next day, I had a meeting with my oncology team to get the bone marrow biopsy results to see if the pediatric chemotherapies had been effective. My oncologist reluctantly had to give me the death speech. She had got to know my entire family and was crying when she spoke those familiar words, "Unfortunately, you did not respond to the pediatric chemotherapies and you are going to die. The hospital is releasing you to go home and spend time with your family and enjoy what time you have left on earth." She mentioned that there was a clinical trial for patients who were just like me where all chemotherapies had failed, and the trial was showing positive results. The trial was for the drug Blinatumomab. I felt compassion for her knowing I was not going to die, and I told her that no matter what happens, everything is going to be all right. I thanked her for her love and honesty.

The next day, we packed up and drove back to Austin with my mom and sister. During the drive, I remember talking to God and explaining to him that I had exhausted all Western medicines known to treat leukemia. I'm sure he smiled, thinking, *Like I don't know that*. I told him that I wasn't sure how he was going to save me but that I knew that he was. I was at peace and could not wait to get home to see my son.

It was good to be home again and see my family. My sister and I spent quality time together and it felt great to be around her again. We would go outside daily for twenty minutes to get some sun. The sun felt very healing but would also drain my energy if I stayed too long. It was mosquito season, and I could see them flying around everywhere. The funny thing was the mosquitoes avoided me like the plague. My body and blood were so toxic from the chemotherapies that I felt like I was glowing. The mosquitoes recognized it and stayed far away.

I continued going to the gym daily to workout and sit in the sauna. One day while I was training, a woman that I did not know approached me and said she had a message to give me. I looked withered and bald from the chemotherapy treatments and was feeling a little rough. I asked her if the message was from Jesus. She looked surprised and said yes it was. She said Jesus told her to speak the verse Isaiah 41:10 directly to me.

Isaiah 41:10 says, "So do not fear, for I am with you; do not be dismayed, for I am your God. I will strengthen you and help you; I will uphold you with my righteous right hand."

I thanked her and gave her a big hug. That verse reaffirmed God's love for me and gave me confidence to stay strong and positive.

Soon after returning from Nashville, a colleague reached out to me and said he wanted me to meet a friend of his that could possibly help with my cancer situation. I was very open minded to any alternative methods of curing cancer and would have tried anything to find the cure. The way I saw it was God was going to bring me the cure, so I met with his friend. His name was Ken Russel. He had created a pink magnesium lotion that contained the vitamin thiamine. The lotion induced an insulin signaling, heavy metal chelating response. In turn, this would help clean my blood and prevent muscle wasting from the chemotherapy. This was fantastic because chemotherapy destroys red blood cells, dumping the contents of the cells into the blood stream. The contents include hemoglobin, which is iron, and overloads the body with toxic heavy metals. This can be detrimental to the organs of the body and cause them to shut down. I started applying the lotion head to toe, twice a day.

My original oncologist, Dr. Juan Posada, called and explained there was a new way to use a chemotherapy I had already tried that had failed. The new way involved bathing the chemotherapy in lipids (fat) and then introducing it into the body. The hope was the leukemia would recognize the chemotherapy as a fat molecule and ingest it, resulting in programed cell death, known as apoptosis. The drug was called liposomal vincristine. I was excited to try it in hopes of achieving remission of the leukemia.

Once again, I had another bone marrow biopsy to determine the level of leukemia in my marrow before starting the new chemotherapy. Surprisingly, the leukemia had dropped from 30 percent to 20 percent just by using the pink magnesium lotion twice a day.

It was Christmas season, and I began the therapy in the outpatient clinic at the Central Texas VA hospital. The protocol was I would have one infusion a week for eight weeks. The chemotherapy was much easier to handle this time because I was applying the pink magnesium lotion, and it was filtering out the overabundance of iron in my blood and helping prevent muscle wasting. I had no horrible side effects.

There were several patients in the outpatient clinic that I would talk to while having my infusion. One patient had a type of blood cancer known as acute promyelocytic leukemia. He was receiving arsenic to kill his leukemia. This made me think of the vitamin B-17 that I had taken before going to Nashville to take the pediatric chemotherapies. I began to wonder if the vitamin B-17 had been responsible for reducing my leukemia from 90 percent to 30 percent.

During Christmas season, I took my son to look at Christmas lights in Belton, Texas. There was a beautiful display of lights along a path that we followed in my truck. Halfway through the course, there was a store where we could stop and buy hot chocolate and gifts and have our picture with Santa Claus. After stocking up on goodies, we walked back to my truck. My son wanted to race back to my vehicle to see who could win. The race was on. I gave him a little head start just to be fair. As I started to run, my body tilted backward in order to be able to raise my feet off the ground. It was like my feet weighed a ton. I felt like I was wearing Bozo the Clown shoes. I realized the effects of the chemotherapy were now causing me to have foot drop type of symptoms. This occurs due to the demyelination effects of chemotherapy has on the nervous system. It eats away the fatty outer covering of the nerves, not allowing nerve signals to be as effective.

I had eight rounds of the new chemotherapy and another bone marrow biopsy to determine its effectiveness. Unfortunately, the new chemotherapy failed, and I still had 20 percent leukemia in my marrow. I continued to use the pink magnesium lotion and go to the gym daily to exercise and sit in the sauna. I also ate very healthy and consumed no processed sugars.

My oncologist Dr. Juan Posada contacted the pharmaceutical company Amgen to discuss the results of their new drug Blinatumomab. The clinical trial had just ended, and it showed promising results. In the clinical trial, 41 percent of the leukemia patients were able to achieve remission. This was exciting news and I hoped that I would be able to try the drug. Representatives from Amgen came to the VA hospital to determine if I was a candidate. Fortunately, I met all requirements and we set a date to begin the treatment in April 2015.

The new drug was different than any other drug I had tried. The new technology used my own cytotoxic killer T cells to destroy the leukemia. The drug operated in two phases and was called a bispecific T-cell engager. Molecularly, the drug looked like a circle with two appendages exiting out of it. One appendage would attach to a leukemia cell and the other appendage would attach to a cytotoxic killer-T cell. The killer-T cells are responsible for recognizing cancer and killing it. Once the leukemia cell and killer T cell were attached, the appendages would approximate, bringing the two cells face to face. The type of leukemia I was fighting had a cloaking mechanism. It had the ability to hide from my killer T cells. This drug brought the two cells close enough together that my killer T cells were able to recognize it as cancer and kill it.

By this time, I had tried all known chemotherapies to treat leukemia and they had all failed. My excitement to try new drugs had diminished, and I wasn't looking forward to the side effects of this drug. I knew God was going to save me, but I did not know how. I had to try this drug to see if this was the way that God was going to use to kill my cancer. If this new drug did not work, I would try the next option that came my way. I knew that God was truth and that he would keep his word to me that I would not die. I knew that one way or another, I would eventually be cancer free.

To administer the new drug, I had to be in the ICU so the doctors could be ready to treat any life-threatening side effects. Per protocol, I was allowed two convulsions before discontinuing the treatment. This worried me because I had never had a convulsion and wasn't sure what to expect. Another very serious side effect was the cytokine response that my body would undergo because of the drug. Cytokines signal immune cells such as T-cells and macrophages to travel to site of infection, which in my case, was the entire body. Cytokines activate other cytokines, stimulating them to produce more cytokines. This produces a cytokine storm, resulting in high fever, swelling, redness, extreme fatigue, nausea, and death.

I had continued to use the pink magnesium lotion and brought several bottles with me to the ICU. I knew the lotion would be extremely beneficial in reducing the effects of the cytokine response. I applied several applications of the pink magnesium lotion the day I entered the hospital to start the new treatment. The Blinatumomab was a twenty-eight-day continuous infusion. It was started in the evening in hopes that I would sleep through the first eight hours. It wasn't long before the cytokine response began to occur. My skin was flush with redness and I spiked a fever. I became nauseous and vomited a few times. The ICU doctor phoned the oncologist who was on call. The oncologist discontinued the treatment for a few hours and restarted it in the morning. After the first day, everything was just fine. After the fourth day in the ICU, I was moved to a private room. This was such a blessing because the ICU is very noisy with screams for help by the staff and yelling from patients with different problems. It was quite the experience.

After nine days in the hospital, I was allowed to go home to finish my twenty-eight-day continuous infusion. I wore an applicator device around my waist, and it fed the drug through a PICC line in my arm. Once home, I immediately went to the gym. I loved the gym and it made me feel alive when I would get my blood pumping. I started working out with weights at age eight and had never stopped. The gym was a place of healing for me. It had always been there, in good times and bad. I mentally and physically always felt better after going.

During the twenty-eight-day infusion, I began to feel better and better. I started to get stronger in my workouts. This drug was nothing like the other chemotherapies I had tried. I was having no side effects and began to wonder if I was getting a placebo. I finished the twenty-eight-day infusion and had another bone marrow biopsy. My oncologist called a few days later and said those magical words that all cancer patients long to hear, "You have reached remission." He was very excited to give me the great news. I was happy but not surprised at all. I knew God was going to save me, and

I guessed this was how he was going to do it. I thanked my oncologist for giving me the fantastic news and I called my family and let everyone know. I had let a few family members know that God spoke to me and said I wasn't going to die, but even they were skeptical after so many failed attempts by my doctors. When God speaks to you, you will know, and it is up to you to believe it at all costs. You must believe it even when you are on the verge of dying day after day, month after month. I had to reassure myself countless times that I was not going to die because it was the will of God.

Once in remission, my oncologist alerted the National Bone Marrow Registry, so they could find a matching donor. It is best to have a family member donate their stem cells if they are a match for you. Unfortunately, no one in my family was a match so the National Bone Marrow Registry found an unrelated donor. They found a twenty-one-year-old male that was a perfect match for me. The donor met ten out of ten criteria for achieving the best results. While they were collecting the donor's stem cells, I had another twenty-eight-day infusion of Blinatumomab to keep me in remission.

I flew back to Nashville in mid-July 2015 to prepare to have the stem cell transplant at the VA/Vanderbilt hospital. In order to get my body ready for transplant, I would be getting ten times the amount of chemotherapy that I had previously been given and six sessions of total body irradiation. Each session of total body irradiation involved sitting in front of the radiation machine for a ten-minute exposure to the front of the body and then a ten-minute exposure to the back of the body. The sanctuary for leukemia in males is the brain and testicles. The radiation treatments included one direct exposure to the testicles to ensure no leukemia was missed. I was told I would be sterile after the radiation treatments. I already had one son, so I was fine with the effects of the treatment. I had another bone marrow biopsy to make sure I was still in remission before the radiation and chemotherapy were given.

The protocol for the total body irradiation was I would receive two sessions a day for three days. I was informed I would be unable to walk after the third session due to lack of blood and energy. I was a little nervous but always remembered God's promise to me. I began the regimen weighing 210 pounds and was in good shape despite all the other failed chemotherapies I had tried. I was lean with my abdominal muscles showing and was ready for the fight of my life.

The bone marrow transplant facility was specially equipped to prevent unwanted pathogens from entering the area. To enter the area, one would have to walk through a sliding glass door up to another sliding glass door. The initial sliding glass door would have to close and the air in between the two doors would be sucked out and new clean air would be pumped in. The second sliding glass door would then open allowing access to the transplant area. All rooms were equipped with negative pressure so air would blow outward when the doors were opened. Food trays were delivered through a double door enclosure from the hallway to the room. All staff wore masks and gloves when entering the patient rooms. Transplant patients would live in the facility fourteen days after the transplant to be closely monitored by the staff. If all went well, the patients would be released to an outside apartment next to the hospital for the next ninety days while recovering.

One the first day of radiation treatment, I was wheeled down to the treatment room. I did not know what to expect so I stayed in prayer. I sat on a bicycle seat with my arms raised above my head as I held on to handles. The treatment began and I did not feel anything. I just heard the sound off the machine. During the treatment, I prayed that the radiation would kill the leukemia and do no long-lasting harm. After my front and back side was complete, I was wheeled back to my room. I remember thinking that this was not bad at all. I returned for the second treatment that afternoon and all went well. I slept well that night and was expecting to wake up unable to walk due to weakness. Morning arrived and I was feeling fine and ready to get the next session underway. I explained to the hospital technicians that I could walk to the treatment room, but they insisted I was wheeled. Both treatments that days went as expected and I slept fine that evening. On the third day, I felt more energized than ever. I was not weak at all. The day went as planned and all was well. I continued to stay in prayer in each session. I remember speaking to the radiation, telling it to do its job and nothing else. I was very confident because God had spoken to me and I knew I wasn't going to die.

On the fourth day, I had the testicular treatment. It lasted a couple of minutes and was painless. During the treatment, the staff played music so the patients could listen and not think about the procedures. The song "Tiny Dancer" by Elton John began playing. A sense of peace fell upon me and I smiled. I will forever associate this song with that point in my life. Every time I hear it now, I get a little choked up as it takes me back to that time in my life where God surrounded me with his love.

The next day, I was given chemotherapy. This dose was ten times stronger than any dose I had previously taken. This is to ensure complete death of all bone marrow and blood so the new stem cells could engraft and proliferate. The following day was a day of rest to allow the chemotherapy to take effect.

The next day, I was given the unrelated donor's stem cells. I was excited and nervous at the same time. I had already had numerous blood and plasma transfusions and was knowledgeable of the side effects that came along with them. I mentally prepared myself through prayer and fasting. The hospital would not allow any food to be eaten before the transplant in order to minimize complications if they should occur. This made it very easy to fast.

The doctors and nurses brought the stem cells in and prepared them to be infused. My nurse and I said a prayer that God would allow the stem cells to be engrafted and my body would accept them without resistance. The nurse started the infusion, and after a couple of hours, the procedure was complete. I was very happy that there were no side effects and that the process went smooth.

I was started on very high doses of steroids to prevent infection. The effects of the steroids were horrible. I was very short tempered and became annoyed with things that would not normally bother me. The lining of my throat to my stomach and all the way down to my anus became ulcerated and peel away. This made it very difficult to swallow and use the restroom. The lining of my small intestine, called microvilli, sloughed off, making it nearly impossible to absorb any food I managed to swallow. I was in such pain that my body produced groanings that I had never heard before or since. I had horribly painful diarrhea to an extent I had never experienced before. I learned to swallow at an extremely slow pace in order to eat. If I could not swallow, there was the option to be fed by a gastric tube. I took pain medication which took the edge off the pain and allowed me to continue to swallow very slowly. I had never been more miserable in my life. Over the next ten days, I constantly reminded myself that God was not going to allow me to die. My blood type changed from A- to AB+. I had no idea one could change blood types.

The combination of total body irradiation coupled with ten times the amount of chemotherapy, killed all my blood, dumping the contents of the cells into my blood stream. This produces iron overload, making my body very toxic. I increased the usage of the pink magnesium lotion to five times a day in order to flush out the heavy metals. The lotion also contains chromium picolinate, which helps the body chelate heavy metals. The insulin signaling properties of the lotion helped prevent muscle wasting even though I was not able to eat much of anything due to the ulcers and sloughing off the mucosal lining of my throat and gut.

During this time, the hospital was under construction directly above the transplant hall. Construction workers were drilling into the concrete above my room. This was very irritating to all the transplant patients and the steroids only intensified the irritability. I remember hearing patients yelling and screaming to have the construction stopped. I was on the verge of snapping. One transplant patient ran out of the air-protected area into the regular hospital just to escape the sound. Thankfully, the hospital staff realized what was happening and stopped the construction. My back hurt from being in bed for long periods, and I would have given anything to have a chiropractic adjustment and a massage. My faith was being tested and this was another time that I had to remind myself I was not going to die because God is true and faithful to his word.

James 1:2–3 (NIV) says, "Consider it pure joy, my brothers and sisters, whenever you face trials of many kinds, 3 because you know that the testing of your faith produces perseverance."

A potentially life-threatening complication of having an unrelated donor stem cell transplant is a reaction called Graft Verses Host Disease (GVHD). This is where the body and the unrelated stem cells fight against each other causing the organs to shut down. GVHD shows up on the skin as little red dots. A little GVHD is good as it shows the transplant has a chance of working. A lot of GVHD is a serious situation which can lead to organ failure and death. It must be monitored very closely and treated with high levels of anti-rejection medication. I ended up having 90 percent GVHD all over my body and my transplant team was very worried. I was treated with very high levels of anti-rejection medication and was given medicated creams to apply to my body to keep the GVHD under control. After a month, the reaction started to calm down and all was well.

My mother was my caregiver throughout my fight with leukemia. She would sleep in my room on a makeshift bed. She would wake up every morning at 2:30 a.m. and go to the hotel where she was staying and prepare my meals for the day. I would not recommend eating the hospital food unless it is healthy and organic. My mother took exceptional care of me. She was very worried about me and did not want to leave my side. She prayed over me daily. This was a special bonding time for us. I had not spent this much time around her since I was a youth. At times, I was very miserable and wasn't nice to her, but she understood. It is part of being a parent and caregiver. I will cherish this time I spent with her forever.

I began having nightmares due to the side effects of the medication I was taking. After a few days of this, I found myself not wanting to go to sleep for fear of having more bad dreams. I prayed to God and asked him how I could prevent myself from having nightmares. That same morning, I was watching Dr. Tony Evans on television. He was preaching about the six pieces of armor of God. He said that whatever was plaguing people originated in the spiritual realm and that we should pray and put on the six pieces of armor on in order to fight spiritual warfare. He defined prayer as earthly permission for heavenly intervention. So I prayed every night and every morning and put on the six pieces of armor of God. My prayer is as follows: "Father God in heaven, I put on your belt of truth because you are faithful and true to your word. I put on your breastplate of righteousness because Christ is righteous and through him, I am saved. I put on your shoes of peace because even though I am being attacked by hell, you give me peace beyond all understanding. I pick up your shield of faith to extinguish all the fiery darts of the evil one. I pick up your helmet of salvation to bring my thinking in line with you father God in heaven. I take up the sword of the spirit, which is your word father God, to advance on the enemy." If I said this prayer before I went to sleep, I did not have nightmares. It was a wonderful discovery and I use it daily.

As the days passed, I slowly started feeling better. I even attempted to do pushups off the end of my bed. My oncologist walked in when I was doing the pushups and demanded I stop. He said I could get another brain bleed from straining. I remember how bad the last brain bleed was and I immediately stopped. I thanked him, and he shook his head and smiled.

I had made friends with the nursing staff in the isolation department. They knew I was a chiropractor and they all had neck and upper back pain. I would go to the nurse's station and, one by one, give them spinal adjustments. It was fantastic to be able to help others who were helping me. There is something that is very healing to the body when you help others. Try it sometime, it may just save your life.

After fourteen days in isolation, I was released to stay at the Vanderbilt apartments located next to the hospital. This was an exciting time for me. Vanderbilt is a very busy area with lots of action located in downtown Nashville. The apartments had an inhouse gym which I used daily. My mother would accompany me and lift weights and walk on the treadmill. I had to be very careful as I was always short of breath and light-headed. I would sit down in between sets of weight lifting in order to not pass out. It felt so good to get my blood flowing and stretch my muscles.

One day while walking on the treadmill, I began to have calf pain. I recognized it immediately and knew it was another blood clot. I had an ultrasound to confirm that it was in fact a blood clot and was started on Lovenox injections in the abdomen twice daily to prevent further clotting. I had hundreds of Lovenox injections prior to this and knew that the clots would eventually dissolve. I continued to workout with weights but had to stop walking on the treadmill until the clots were gone.

It had been six weeks since I had seen my son and I was missing him very badly. I would Skype with him daily, and this helped to be able to see him and hear his voice. I longed to hold him tight and kiss him and love on him. Not being around him was very difficult and I had to control my emotions in fear of developing a negative attitude and becoming depressed. Death was still nipping at my heels and would take advantage of any weakness to bring me down.

Several of the patients that had gone through the stem cell transplant that I had become friends with had already died due to infection or other complications. Knowing this could cause one to second-guess God's word and lead to depression and a downward spiral. Staying positive at the most difficult times is a must and I achieved this by incessant prayer and thanking God for my trials and tribulations.

Romans 5:3–5 says, "Not only that, but we rejoice in our sufferings knowing that suffering produces endurance, and endurance produces character, and character produces hope, and hope does not put us to shame, because God's love has been poured into our hearts through the Holy Spirit who has been given to us."

Early in my fight with cancer, a childhood friend, Ryan Butler, reached out to me. We had grown up together in Amarillo and he was now a captain in the military, stationed at Aberdeen Proving Ground in Maryland. He would send me daily biblical scriptures late at night so they would be ready for me to read first thing in the morning. This would help me by getting my focus on God before starting the day. I looked forward to this every morning and still do to this day. Ryan retired from the military around the time I was recovering from the stem cell transplant. He had to drive through Nashville on his way back to Texas. We met at Cracker Barrel for breakfast. It was great to see him and his wife. After breakfast, they prayed a wonderful prayer over me and got on their way. Captain Butler has been faithful in sending me God's word daily for five years and continues to do so.

My other sister Angie and her daughters came to visit me. It had been years since I had seen them, and they were grown up now. They looked at me a little strange as I was bald and withered. They were accustomed to seeing me as a two-hundred-fifty-pound muscular man and now I was skinny and frail. They all gave me big hugs and love which was healing to my body and soul. It was lobster season, so we went to Red Lobster to indulge. Even though I could not taste anything due to the side effects of radiation, I still cleaned my plate. The dish looked so good, and I bet it tasted wonderful.

Toward the end of my one-hundred-day recovery, my mother returned home, and my father flew to Nashville to be my caregiver. It was great to see him. I got him to start working out with me and get in better shape. He would typically golf daily back home, and he was turning over a new leaf by weight training. This was special bonding time for us. We walked around the Vanderbilt campus, exploring areas and buying many unnecessary gifts and souvenirs. Being around your parents day in and day out as an adult allows everyone to get to know each other on a deeper level. I will cherish this time with him forever.

It had now been close to three months since I had seen my son and I was missing him very much. My family scheduled a trip for him to fly to Nashville so I could finally get to see him and love on him. I was so excited I could hardly wait. The day before he was scheduled to come see me, he contracted a cold and spiked a fever. We had to cancel his trip because I had no immune system and was still very vulnerable to getting sick. This broke my heart and I became a little depressed. I was aware that any negativity could send me into a tailspin, so I prayed about it got over it. I was too close to going home to allow my emotions to get the best of me. I knew I would get to see my son in a month or so. After all, I still got to see him on Skype and hear his voice daily.

I was recovering faster than expected and was released to go home early. Instead of staying the usual one hundred days after transplant, I was allowed to go home on day 88. Mentally, this was very helpful as I could not wait to see my son. We packed up and drove back to Austin the next day.

It was October 20, 2015, when my father and I left Nashville and started the journey home. The weather was beautiful, and the countryside was arrayed with different types of trees, full of majestic colors. Everything was new to me. The colors of the landscape were breath taking. The sounds of the birds and the blowing of the wind were healing to my mind and body. Different smells brought back memories of good times. I was so excited and in such a good mood, I thought I was going to explode.

I had not told my son I was coming home early, and I could not wait to surprise him at school the next day. My father and I stopped in Little Rock, Arkansas, for the night. This was the first time I had been that far away from my transplant team and was a little nervous if something went wrong. That night, we ate a fantastic dinner and fell asleep. During the night, I woke up and felt hot and dehydrated. I started to panic, knowing that dehydration is a death sentence for patients recovering from a transplant. It was crazy how in just a few hours I could go from feeling fantastic to feeling like my organs were shutting down. I realized that during the eight-hour road trip, I had not kept up with my hydration. I remembered seeing a VA hospital sign on the way into town and was considering having my father take me in. I knew that if we went to the hospital, they would admit me, and I would be there for a few days to rehydrate. I became determined to find a solution myself. I would only drink very clean water, and it was in my truck outside of the hotel. My father was sleeping heavily, and I did not want to wake him, so I grabbed the keys and stumbled to the truck. After getting to the water, I downed several liters. The water had never tasted so good. It was like I was drinking life back into my body. After an hour of consuming water, I began to feel much better and fell back to sleep. In the morning when I woke up, everything was back to normal. We ate a good breakfast and got back on the road for the remaining five-hour trip.

Halfway home, we stopped at a rest area to stretch our legs and throw away trash. When my father stepped out of my truck, his foot caught the edge of the curb and he fell. Luckily, his wrestling skills from high school kicked in and tucked and rolled. When he stood up, he was grabbing his shoulder where he had a shoulder replacement a year prior. I could tell he was in pain and asked if he wanted to go to the hospital. He declined as all he could think about was getting me to see my son. Over the next couple of hours, his shoulder began to swell all the way up to his throat. I was worried it would affect his breathing, but he was persistent in getting me home. Jokingly, he said he was just going to rub some dirt on it and everything would be fine. I knew there was a fracture, but I was not sure where. My father is a strong and tough man and can endure a lot of pain. The next day, an x-ray confirmed that he had fractured his clavicle, but his shoulder replacement had not been damaged.

Upon arriving back in Austin, my stepmother met us at my son's school. She was very worried about my dad but was willing to postpone taking him to the hospital in order to see my son's face when I surprised him. We waited in the front office for him while a phone call was made to his third-grade class. He was told to come to the principal's office and was not given a reason. I hid behind a small plant. My father and Jill, a.k.a. Papa and Gigi, stood out in the open. When he walked through the door, he was excited thinking I would be there. After he did not see me, his shoulders slumped, and he toughed out a smile. I have a specific whistle that rhymes with his first two names, Michael David. I made this whistle, and he immediately turned around to see who was whistling his name. He was so surprised to see me. My heart was beating so fast and I was trembling with joy. I could not wait to hold him in my arms. He ran over to me, and I picked him up in my arms and held him so tight. He was holding me tighter than he ever had, and I will always remember than wonderful feeling of love.

My son and I moved into a two-bedroom apartment so I could continue with the long recovery. My lungs had been severely damaged throughout the past year and I was always short of breath. Every time I stood up, I would feel like I was going to pass out. I would stand up out of my recliner and immediately lay down on the ottoman to prevent myself from passing out. Once I was stable, I would stand back up and hang on to the arm on the couch in a bent-over position until it was safe to start walking. This lasted a year and still has not completely gone away.

As I physically improved, I could feel God's presence lessoning. He had kept me so close during my journey with cancer that I became accustomed to having him there and feeling him as if he was cuddling me. Now I felt him gently nudging me back into the world so I could continue with being his servant and helping others. It is a little odd, but I miss those times when I was close to death because God's presence was so overwhelming. I could feel his love pressing in on me to the point that it was almost paralyzing and the hair on my body would stand on its end.

I started the process of returning to normal life. I had to suddenly leave my chiropractic business eighteen months earlier and needed to file for bankruptcy. December 2015, I went to court and explained my situation and the court declared me bankrupt. This was a big financial burden that was lifted off my shoulders, and I could now focus on reestablishing myself as a chiropractor and helping others.

That same month, my son and I auditioned for a Screen Actor's Guild Reliant Energy commercial and landed the job. It was wonderful to be able to act with my son for the first time. To top it off, Matthew McConaughey provided the voiceover for the commercial. Our commercial is now on YouTube under Kelly and Kelly Reliant Energy Commercial. We continue to audition together and, as of 2019, shot a Facebook commercial. These acting jobs make great memories and is something we can always go back and watch. I took my first acting class at Tyler Junior College in 1993 and had pursued acting ever since. I had a guest star appearance on Walker Texas Ranger and had small scenes with Chuck Norris, Clarence Gilyard, and John Savage. I also had a small scene with Mickey Rourke in a movie that was shot in Dallas, Texas.

A lot of my patients from my chiropractic clinic had followed me on Facebook during my journey with cancer. Now that I was home, they began to ask if I was back in practice. I set up a chiropractic table in the living room of my apartment and began giving spinal adjustments. My patients are my friends, and they were happy to see me alive and improving. I was still very weak and short of breath. I would need to take rest breaks while adjusting different parts of their spines. They were understanding of my situation and worked with me while I cared for them. It was a wonderful feeling to be back in practice and helping others. I was receiving healing by helping others with their aches and pains.

My body was toxic from the chemotherapy which continued to hang around in my fat cells. I knew the only way to completely get rid of it was to lose all of my body fat. Losing body fat is a difficult process, and the lower the body fat percent gets, the harder it is to lose. In order to ensure I got rid of the chemotherapy, I had to lose most of my body fat. I had leaned out a few times in the past to compete in bodybuilding competitions and knew it was extremely both mentally and physically. There was an all-natural bodybuilding competition coming up in June 2016 called the Texas Shredder Classic in Austin. I signed up for it and started the leaning out process in April 2016. This competition gave me a goal and time limit to get ready. My body was wasted from the stem cell transplant, but I was determined to get the chemotherapy out of my system. The key for me to get lean was to do fasted cardio early in the morning and in the afternoon, I would do weight training followed with more cardio. I maintained a strict diet and monitored my proteins, carbohydrates, and fats. I was taking oral chemotherapy daily and several other medications for cancer and this made it harder to get lean. As long as I stayed in prayer, I could finish the daily training schedule. Cardio was much more difficult as my lungs were compromised from the damage caused by radiation, chemotherapy, and blood clots. I stayed focused on the goal which was to rid my body of the chemotherapy trapped in my fat cells.

The day of the competition arrived, and I was ready. My son and parents were seated close to the front to give me support. I had a spray tan applied over my body to accentuate the separation of the muscles, and I was ready to step on stage. I was forty-four years old and entered the open division, which is all ages, and the master's division. I won second place in the open division and second place in the master's division. I left with two trophies and was very pleased.

The next morning, I awoke to red dots all over my body. The spray tan had choked off my skin, which is the largest organ of the body, and kicked my graft versus host disease into full gear. I felt horrible and could not believe I had not thought of that beforehand. It took four months to calm down, and eventually I returned to normal. Needless to say, that was my last bodybuilding competition.

Conclusion

There were several times that I thought I was going to die during my fight with leukemia and the treatments that go along with it. I do not think I would have had the mental strength to continue on if God had not spoken to me and told me I was not going to die. I relied completely on his word and believed what he told me, especially when my oncologists said I was going to die. Daily, I spoke out loud, "God, I trust you." I was content in living or dying because I gave my situation over to God. I was too weak to fight, and God's grace alone saved me.

Second Corinthians 12:9–10 says, "But he said to me, "My grace is sufficient for you, for my power is made perfect in weakness." Therefore I will boast all the more gladly of my weakness, so that the power of Christ may rest upon me. For the sake of Christ, then, I am content with weakness, insults, hardships, persecutions, and calamities. For when I am weak, then I am strong."

I want to give a special thanks to those people who sign up with the National Bone Marrow Registry. You truly help save lives. I also want to thank people who donate blood. I had countless blood and plasma transfusions and you saved my life. I want to thank my oncologists, nurses, my bone marrow transplant team, chaplains, the staff who kept my hospital rooms super clean, the food delivery personnel, social workers, the VA, Vanderbilt Hospital, and Baylor Scott and White

Hospital for all that you do for people in need. Thank you, Regina Thomas, for giving me love by gently rubbing my neck and shoulders during the fifteen bone marrow biopsies I received at the VA. Thank you to the people who mailed me get-well cards and others who sent me countless encouraging messages on social media. It truly makes a big difference to know that people care and are praying for you.

It takes years to recover from chemotherapy, total body irradiation, and a stem cell transplant. I have not recovered to the point where I was before cancer, but I do appreciate what I have remaining after the good fight. My lungs are compromised, and I am still occasionally short of breath. I have half of the strength as I did before, but I still feel and look good. I am grateful to be alive and can raise my son. I will never take another day for granted. I thank God every morning for allowing me to wake up and enjoy his grace and mercy. I am truly blessed considering the alternative. Even on my worst days, God gave me peace which surpasses all understanding.

I was fasting and praying to father God in heaven asking him what he wanted me to title this book. He simply replied, "Be Still and Know That I Am God."

About the Author

Dr. Michael Alton II is a native Texan, born in Amarillo. He has dedicated his life to helping others. He began his medical career in the United States Army as a combat medic. He has a Bachelor of Science in Nursing from Texas A&M, Corpus Christi. He earned his Doctorate of Chiropractic from Cleveland Chiropractic College of Los Angeles.

Dr. Alton empathetically understands his patient's pain through first-hand experience, having suffered a fractured spine while in the military. Later in life, he was diagnosed with two types of leukemia and also suffered a stroke.

His God-given wisdom, knowledge, and understanding allows him to treat his patients very effectively with compassion at any age or stage of life.

Dr. Alton is a servant of God and his purpose in life is to heal others and give them the best quality of life possible.